P9-CMQ-508

BLAIRSVILLE SENIOR HIGH SCHOOL
BLAIRSVILLE, PENNA.

Terror and Treasure

by Kathryn Long Humphrey

SHIPWRECKS

Franklin Watts
New York • London • Toronto • Sydney
A First Book • 1991

19001

*For my son, Rich,
with oceans
of good wishes*

Photographs copyright ©: The Mary Rose Trust: pp. 8, 10, 17, 19, 20, 22, 23; Giraudon/Art Resource Inc., N.Y.: p. 12; Stan Waterman: pp. 25, 30, 32, 33, 35, 36; Woods Hole Oceanographic Institution, MA.: pp. 39, 41 bottom, 55; New York Public Library, Picture Collection: pp. 41 top, 47, 50, 54; The Mariners' Museum, VA.: pp. 43, 45, 53.

Library of Congress Cataloging-in-Publication Data

Humphrey, Kathryn Long.
    Shipwrecks : terror and treasure / by Kathryn Long Humphrey.
        p.   cm.—(A First book)
    Includes bibliographical references and index.
    Summary: Examines the discovery and exploration of three shipwrecks, the Mary Rose, Concepcion, and Titanic.
    ISBN 0-531-20031-0
    1. Shipwrecks—Juvenile literature. 2. Underwater exploration—Juvenile Literature.   [1. Shipwrecks. 2. Underwater exploration.] I. Title. II. Series.
G525.H897   1991
930.1'028'04—dc20   91-16962 CIP AC

COPYRIGHT © 1991 BY KATHRYN LONG HUMPHREY
ALL RIGHTS RESERVED
PRINTED IN THE UNITED STATES OF AMERICA
6 5 4 3 2

Contents

Introduction

Before airplanes became popular, people often traveled by ship across dangerous seas, rivers, and lakes. Thousands of ships were wrecked and lost.

Twentieth-century scientists have since developed *scuba* diving equipment and robots. They invented *sonar,* which reflects sound waves off of undersea vessels, and *magnetometers,* which locate large amounts of metal underwater. These inventions have helped men and women discover shipwrecks with treasures from the past.

Chapter 1
King Henry's Warship

Before dawn on Sunday, July 19, 1545, the English wooden warship, the *Mary Rose,* prepared to battle the French. Cannons and heavy guns were hoisted into position. The crew fastened nets over the *decks* to keep the French from sneaking on board and fighting man to man.

France wanted to destroy England's main naval base at Portsmouth and the sixty ships anchored there. Two hundred thirty-five French ships and 30,000 Frenchmen headed for England.

England's king, Henry VIII (Henry the Eighth), stood on the shore near Southsea Castle. While the warships fought at sea, Henry would lead soldiers to battle on land.

Henry could see his favorite ship, the *Mary Rose.* It

was built in 1510, when he was still a teenage king. He named it after his sister, Princess Mary. In 1536, he ordered shipbuilders to mount cannons and heavy guns on the lower decks. With the larger guns, men could shoot rocks and iron balls long distances.

These weapons made the *Mary Rose* a new kind of fighting ship for the 1500s. Before that time, English sailors had fought sea battles by getting close to enemy ships and climbing on board. Then they shot arrows or fired guns at their enemies or attacked them head-on with long, pointed weapons called *pikes*.

In 1545 the crew of the *Mary Rose* could still fight man to man. Archers and pikemen were on board. The archers could jump on enemy ships and fight, or stay on the *Mary Rose* and shoot their bows and arrows long distances.

English archers were the best in the world, and they terrified the French. English boys began practicing archery when they were young. The law required that fathers give their sons a bow and arrows when they were seven years old.

Outstanding bowmen could shoot an arrow every five seconds, and they could shoot them as great a distance as 300 yards (274 m), the length of three football fields.

Besides pikemen and archers, the *Mary Rose* carried many other people. Some wore heavy armor. But not all of the seven hundred were warriors. Carpenters,

Almost 450 years ago, this cannon
fired at the French from the deck
of the *Mary Rose*. It now stands
in the *Mary Rose* Museum in
Portsmouth, England.

cooks, a barber-surgeon (in the 1500s, doctors were also barbers), and men to run the ship were on board, too.

These men brought tools for their various tasks. And seamen packed musical instruments and games to help them relax after a hard day's work on the ship. They brought fiddles, drums, and games with dice, such as backgammon. They even carried with them a new game called dominoes, which Henry VIII liked to play.

But that Sunday in July 1545, the seamen were not thinking of games. The battle was about to begin. Someone fired a cannonball. The *Mary Rose,* under the command of Vice Admiral George Carew, prepared to set sail.

But the *Mary Rose* could not budge. Neither could any of the other English ships in the Portsmouth harbor. There was no wind. Square-rigged *carracks* like the *Mary Rose* couldn't sail without a breeze.

The French were not stranded. They had twenty-two small fighting ships called *galleys,* which their sailors could row with oars when the wind didn't blow. The French galleys rowed across part of the *English Channel* called The Solent and shot at the English ships.

An hour later, the wind began to blow. Then the English ships could retaliate and chase the French. The small galleys raced back toward the larger French ships for protection.

Many objects were salvaged from the *Mary Rose*. These flutelike instruments and other objects don't look like they had been under water for centuries.

The *Mary Rose* hoisted her sails. Lids of the *gunports* were raised, and guns rammed through the openings, ready for action. Some guns jetted out only a few inches above the water.

The *Mary Rose* was having trouble. It wasn't operating properly. Admiral George Carew's uncle sailed past the *Mary Rose* in another ship and asked what was wrong.

"I have the sort of *knaves* I cannot rule," Carew shouted in reply. Perhaps what he meant was his officers and crew refused to follow orders.

The *Mary Rose* was so overloaded with guns and men in heavy armor that it was beginning to sink. Its gunports almost touched the waterline. The ship *listed* to one side. Some of the gun openings dipped beneath the water. Someone should have closed the lids to keep the water from seeping in, but no one did. Water rushed in through the open gun holes and began filling the ship. The *Mary Rose* tipped on its side and started to sink.

Two archers from a lower deck tried to climb a ladder to a higher dry spot. But the ladder tipped so much to one side, they toppled off.

Seamen on the top deck tried to jump off the *Mary Rose* to safety. But they were caught in the nets they had strung from side to side to keep the enemy out. Only about three dozen men scrambled free. In less

Henry VIII is pictured here at
age forty-nine. Five years later
he would watch his ship sink and his
troops die in a tragedy that
could have been avoided.

than a minute the *Mary Rose* sank to the bottom of the sea. Not even the ship's rats escaped.

King Henry stared in horror from the shore. Drowning men screamed. Dead bodies floated on the water. Admiral George Carew's wife stood next to the king, and fainted as she watched her husband drown.

"Oh, my gentlemen! Oh, my *gallant* men!" King Henry cried out.

Over six hundred of his men died. His favorite ship sank. Only the tops of two masts of the *Mary Rose* showed above the water.

Chapter 2
Trapped in Time

Nearly 450 years later, in 1981, a scuba diver named Alexander McKee had an eerie feeling as he swam through the *Mary Rose*. The ship was 45 feet (13.7 m) below the surface of the water. A skull with white teeth peered at him. McKee swam past bronze and iron guns still locked into firing position, trapped in time since the day the *Mary Rose* had sunk.

McKee was still a little boy when he first heard about the legendary ship. The *Mary Rose* had been lost since King Henry's reign, although signs of it had been noted around 1590 and 1840. Some people thought the *Mary Rose* had probably rotted away. But McKee didn't agree. He dreamed of finding it.

As McKee grew up, he continued to think about the missing ship. He learned scuba diving and joined an

English diving club called the Sub-Aqua Club. In 1965 he organized a few divers to look for the *Mary Rose* and other sunken ships in the muddy, icy waters near Portsmouth, England.

The group studied old maps and stories about the *Mary Rose*. They decided to search in the area of the English Channel called The Solent. They dived in their spare time, mostly on summer weekends. Margaret Rule joined the divers as a land *archaeologist,* and later learned scuba diving.

McKee's group did not have much money to spend on the search for the *Mary Rose*. Diving clubs loaned them boats, but they had none of the special equipment that would be needed for success. Though they worked long hours, two years later they had still not found the *Mary Rose*. Sometimes they wondered if they ever would.

In 1967 and 1968 Professor Harold Edgarton from the United States demonstrated new underwater equipment in England. This included a *magnetometer,* which finds large amounts of metal under the earth or underwater. He also displayed how *sonar* works by bouncing sound waves off objects. Both instruments can help show the location of unusual objects below the surface.

McKee arranged to borrow the equipment to hunt for the *Mary Rose*. The sonar showed that there was something unusual under the water where they were searching. This gave the divers new hope of finding the ship. The group asked for legal protection against looters in their search area.

They continued diving. In 1970 McKee discovered the barrel of a 430-year-old iron gun used in King Henry's time.

In 1971, the first diver who plunged into the ocean's depths rushed back to report what he saw. Winter storms had blown away some of the sand at the bottom of the sea and uncovered part of a ship.

It was the *Mary Rose*!

News of the ship's discovery spread. People donated money and digging equipment. Divers volunteered to help. Month by month and year by year they slowly cleared away the sand. More and more of the ship showed. Finally, half of the *Mary Rose* was uncovered. The other half had rotted or had been eaten away.

Prince Charles, the Prince of Wales and future King of England, was a scuba diver and wanted to see the *Mary Rose*. On July 30, 1975, he traveled to Portsmouth and joined McKee's group of divers for the day. He became the first royal person to see the ship since King Henry VIII.

Over the next seven years Prince Charles dived to the *Mary Rose* eight more times. The divers could not talk to each other underwater. When Prince Charles wanted to ask a question, he wrote it on a wrist pad. He said that going down in those dark, muddy waters

Divers work on the *Mary Rose* at the bottom of the English Channel.

was like swimming in lentil soup, which is thick like pea soup.

In 1978 people interested in the *Mary Rose* made plans to raise the ship from the water. This giant project would have to be finished within a few years if they wanted to preserve the ship. For more than 400 years a soft blanket of sand had protected the wood from rotting. Once the sand was cleared away, the ship slowly began to weaken. The *Mary Rose* would have to be moved to a place where it could be sprayed with chemicals before it rotted too much.

In 1979, Prince Charles became president of a new group called the *Mary Rose* Trust. Members of the group would take care of the *Mary Rose*. They needed thousands of dollars to lift the *Mary Rose* from the sea and to protect the ship and the items inside it.

Prince Charles gave speeches to help raise money. The group built a museum to house the *Mary Rose* and the objects found in and around it.

Divers slowly vacuumed the soft sand off the ship's decks. As they did, they found treasures from the past which told about life in 1545. They uncovered clothes, food, sailing equipment, and candles. They found so many pocket compasses that archaeologist Margaret Rule thinks they were as popular in the 1500s as wristwatches are today.

They found fiddles, drums, dice, a domino, a chessboard, and backgammon boards with game pieces.

Many people worked on the *Mary Rose* while it was in the sea and when it was raised. It needed to be restored and preserved so visitors would always be able to see Henry VIII's favorite ship.

Sailors brought many objects with them
on their voyage. Here are a comb, rosary
beads, a die, coins, and what looks like a
whistle. These were all found among
the ruins of the *Mary Rose*.

There was a medicine chest that had belonged to the ship's barber-surgeon, or doctor. His finger mark could still be seen in a jar of ointment. The chest held razors, syringes, a pewter bowl for *bloodletting*, and the wooden handle of a saw. The doctor cut off diseased arms and legs with the saw.

A dog's skeleton lay curled in the position it was sleeping in at the time the ship sank. Divers found a frog's skeleton, the bones of a rat, and parts of cockroaches and flies that had bothered sailors nearly 450 years ago.

Two hundred human skeletons were discovered. An officer's skeleton lay on top of what was probably his sword. Gold coins could still be found in the pocket of his trousers. Bones of sailors, and pieces of the net that trapped them were scattered around the top deck. Near the bones of gunners, divers saw the open gunports which had let the water first enter the ship and caused it to sink.

The skeletons of two archers lay next to the ladder that they had tried to climb in their scramble to escape. Scientists who studied the bones learned that one was in his middle twenties and was about 5 feet 7 inches (1.7 m) tall. The other was a 6-foot (1.8 m) twenty-two-year-old. His jerkin, or leather vest, lay beside him, and a leather case of arrows was still slung over his backbone.

Over 2,500 arrows and 139 long bows were found.

After over four centuries of burial at the bottom of the sea, the *Mary Rose* finally rises again to the surface of the water—with a little help from modern technology. Tourists can now visit history on the ship that battled the French and sank in 1545.

Fitted with new strings, many of the bows could still be used today. Leather gloves were found that once protected the archers' hands when they shot flaming arrows.

Divers were still busy clearing the ship in 1982, as the deadline for it to be raised drew near. Finally they finished. On October 11, 1982, the *Mary Rose* was hoisted from the sea on a steel cradle and taken to the ship hall which had been specially built for it in Portsmouth. A year later the hall was opened to the public. People can journey to see the *Mary Rose* for themselves, and over 2 million tourists have done so. The ship is sprayed frequently so it will be preserved.

Visitors in the 1990s get a feeling of what life was like during the reign of Henry VIII.

Chapter 3
Wrecked on a Reef

After Columbus discovered America, Spanish explorers seized as much gold and silver as they could find in the New World. In the sixteenth and seventeenth centuries, treasure ships, called *galleons,* sailed the oceans, carrying riches back to Spain every year.

The galleon *Nuestra Señora de Concepción,* often called simply the *Concepción,* sailed from Cuba with a fleet of ships in 1641. It was loaded with a hundred tons of treasure. Bars of gold and silver were stacked shoulder-high. Hundreds of *pieces of eight*, the most popular silver coins at the time, were stashed on board.

In those days pirates roamed the Caribbean, stealing and killing. But the *Concepción*'s thirty-six bronze cannons and three gun-decks scared off would-be thieves and plunderers. What the admiral feared more than

The *Concepción*'s cannons could only
protect it from human enemies—not
from the storms and reefs that
would determine its destiny.

pirates were the dangerous reefs and tropical storms in the Caribbean.

The *Concepción* sailed past Bermuda. Then a hurricane struck. Winds ripped the *Concepción*'s sails. The old wooden ship sprang several leaks. At any moment, it could fill with water and sink. Day and night the crew scooped out water with buckets and bottles. They could not count on the pumps because they were jammed so often with dirt or gunpowder.

Sailors crawled along the top deck, as the boat tossed and turned, fumbling for cargo to throw off to lighten the ship. Seawater poured over the sides, while howling winds blew.

The storm pounded on the *Concepción* and it was separated from the other ships. Even after the winds began to die down, the ship was tossed around for three more weeks. The seamen were half-starved, and desperate for water. Worst of all, they didn't know in what direction to sail to reach land.

In those days, ships did not have instruments that told their exact position. When the storm finally blew over, the officers didn't know where they were. They argued about their location. The pilots said they were north of Puerto Rico and should head south. But the admiral said they were farther west, and if they sailed south, they would smash into a narrow ridge of coral rocks called a *reef*.

The men kept arguing, but the pilots refused to give

in. Finally the admiral said that they could steer the ship south, but he didn't like the idea. He called for a silver basin and washed his hands in front of everyone. This is how he showed he would not be responsible for what happened.

And what happened was terrible, because the admiral had been right.

At 8:30 on the night of October 30, the *Concepción* slammed into the reef. The ship slumped to one side, holes gashed in it. All night long the ship was pounded against the reef by the waves.

The sailors tried to make the ship lighter so it would slip free of the reef and sail away. They threw cannons and ammunition over the sides. And for a while it looked as if they would escape.

But a new storm slammed the ship back against the reef. The *Concepción* crashed against one rock after another. Finally it jammed. The ship was going to sink.

To save the treasure, the crew tossed pouches and bars of gold and silver on top of the coral reef. They planned to return for this mountain of treasure later.

Some men jumped into the ship's lifeboats. Others tore up boards from the deck to make rafts.

The *Concepción* filled with water. People still on board the ship panicked. Many jumped over the sides and tried to climb on rafts and lifeboats that floated by. But there was not enough room for everyone.

As lifeboats and rafts became crowded, men drew

swords and knives and fought for space. Some even killed priests. Screams filled the air as men fought and died.

One overloaded raft was so low in the sea that water came up to the passengers' waists. Sharks attacked them. Some people were so frightened they went insane.

Pirates robbed passengers on another raft, then put them ashore. Some of the sailors walked to the place that is now called the Dominican Republic.

The main ship, the *Concepción,* was sinking, but many still clung to it. Those who escaped promised to send help. But nearly everyone who stayed on the ship drowned.

Tales spread of a mountain of gold and silver stacked on a reef.

Chapter 4
Diving for Treasure

In the 1970s, an American scuba diver named Burt Webber hoped to find the *Concepción*'s riches. Nearly 300 years earlier the treasure hunter William Phipps had located the *Concepción,* using boats supplied by English noblemen. Phipps took tons of gold and silver from the ship. But people believed millions of dollars' worth of the *Concepción*'s treasure was still buried among the reefs near the Dominican Republic.

Jack Haskins, who worked with Webber in the 1970s, went to Spain to study the reports and letters about the *Concepción.* He hired someone to translate them into English. He also went to England and studied William Phipps's treasure maps. On one map he found the words "Ye Wrack." Webber thought that meant "the wreck." He was sure it marked the spot where the treasure was hidden.

Although William Phipps had found some of
the *Concepción*'s treasure, Webber and his
crew did not search in vain. Here,
a diver shows a brilliant gold chain
he found among the rocks.

Webber raised money for a boat and expensive equipment, including magnetometers. He planned to search for the *Concepción* near the Dominican Republic. In 1977 he hunted for five months, but failed to find the ship.

Webber did not give up.

He raised more money for another boat and better equipment. In November 1978, he and his crew left on a new search. If they found the treasure, the government of the Dominican Republic would get half of it for allowing them to search. The other half would be divided between Webber and those working with him and supplying the funds.

On the fourth day of Webber's treasure hunt, he dived underwater and dug up an olive jar from the coral. It was the same kind of jar that the *Concepción* would have carried.

The next day, another diver, Jim Nace, grabbed a rock from the reef. He pried a round, gray object from it. He wondered if it was a coin and swam to show Webber.

Webber nearly leaped out of the water. He was sure it was a piece of eight. The men swam to the search boat with it. Henry Taylor, an expert on old Spanish objects dropped it into a cleaning solution. When he pulled the coin out, it was silver and shiny. It *was* a piece of eight! The letters OMP stamped on it showed

Webber's team used
state-of-the-art
equipment to search
for the lost ship
and its treasures
on the ocean floor.

it was from an old mint in Mexico. Webber believed it was from the *Concepción*.

Nace and Webber dived back in the water. Instruments gave high readings of metal near an underwater cave, and they began digging there. One piece of eight fell out. Then more appeared. Then a whole stream of coins rolled out. Another diver discovered a stack of coins near a different wall. Soon many divers were finding treasure.

At the end of the day, the team screamed and laughed as they rose to the surface. "We're no longer treasure hunters. We're treasure finders," diver Bob Coffey said later.

The group found more and more treasure. They discovered clumps of coins stuck together in the shape of square wooden chests. The chests had rotted away. One clump of coins weighed 200 pounds (90 kg), and it took three divers to carry it to the surface.

The divers found musket balls, iron spikes, pottery—and more and more coins. One cave was so full of coins the divers called it the money hole.

Even though the ship itself had rotted away, they had found the lost treasure of the *Concepción*!

Three days later, Webber and his team went to the Dominican Republic's naval base in Santo Domingo to ask for protection. The treasure was worth millions of dollars, and Webber was afraid of robbers. The

Coins were found
by the hundreds!

Pieces of eight are spread
across a table for study.

China cups survived the shipwreck, to be
discovered over 300 years later!

Dominican government sent a navy warship to keep pirates away.

Webber returned to the wreck. Divers found several thousand more coins, a gold necklace, silver plates, forks, and candlesticks, and a bronze *astrolabe* made in 1619. Sailors on the *Concepción* used the astrolabe to find the latitude.

Webber believed there was more treasure inside the reefs. The men blasted for it and discovered thousands of more coins, two more astrolabes, and many other valuable objects.

The legend of treasure stacked on a reef was true. Newspaper reports said Webber's discovery was worth between $40 million and $900 million.

Webber gave half of this to the Dominican Republic. Some of the treasure Spanish explorers had stolen was finally returned to people of the New World.

Chapter 5
A Ship Called Unsinkable

On the night of April 14, 1912, lookout Frederick Fleet stood high in the *crow's nest* of the RMS *Titanic*. No moon lit the way, and he strained to see ahead. The ship had received several iceberg warnings. Now it sailed through the iceberg field.

Passengers aboard this ocean liner's first voyage thought nothing could go wrong with the *Titanic*. It was the largest ship in the world. Many said it was the safest. They called it unsinkable. But Fleet remembered the warnings and kept a sharp eye out for floating mountains of ice. No one had remembered to bring binoculars for the lookouts.

Suddenly, in front of the ship, Fleet saw a huge, dark shape. An iceberg! He clanged the ship's bell three times, then phoned the part of the ship called the *bridge*.

The *Titanic*'s wheel sat on this base, but
alas, the ship could not be turned in
time to avoid the iceberg in its path.

When the officer on duty answered, Fleet spoke quickly. "Iceberg dead ahead."

The officer ordered a sharp turn, but it was too late. At 11:40 P.M., the iceberg scraped against the side of the *Titanic*. There was a grinding noise. Then the ship came to a sudden halt.

Many people on board slept through the collision or hardly noticed it. Others thought nothing serious had happened. Some were excited about seeing an iceberg and had ice fights with chunks of it that fell on the deck.

A few passengers kept eating their late dinner or listening to the ship's band. Others played cards. A luxury steamship like the *Titanic* seemed safe.

The ship was a "floating palace." It was four city blocks long and had tennis courts, a kennel for pets, fancy dining rooms, a grand stairway, and a ballroom with chandeliers. And it was the first ship with a swimming pool.

First-class passengers paid more for a ticket from Southampton, England, to New York on the *Titanic* than a new house cost then in New York. Millionaires, such as John Jacob Astor, Isador Strauss, and Benjamin Guggenheim were on board. Archie Butt, advisor to then-President William Taft, was also among the 325 first-class passengers.

Not all the passengers were wealthy or famous. About 285 were in second class, and more than 700

This black-and-white photo shows the luxurious accommodations of first-class passengers aboard the *Titanic*. The color photo shows what remains of the beautiful bed after over seventy years at the bottom of the sea.

were in the less expensive third, or steerage, class in the lower part of the ship. Many steerage passengers were immigrants.

Captain Edward Smith rushed to the bridge from his cabin and asked what the ship had hit. When he heard it was an iceberg, he sent someone below to check. Later, he and shipbuilder Thomas Andrews went to look at the damage for themselves. They saw water gushing in.

The captain knew that the *Titanic* would sink. And worse! He knew there were over 2,200 people on board, and the ship carried only enough lifeboats for about half of them. He should have paid more attention to the warnings and slowed the ship down. The company should have added more lifeboats.

Smith knew that if help did not come in time, he would die that night. He would go down with his ship. But few passengers suspected danger. Everyone said the *Titanic* was unsinkable. It had an extra bottom. And if water started to enter one part of the ship, mechanical walls would go up to make sixteen water-tight compartments. These should keep the water from spreading. Even if four of the compartments flooded, the ship could still float. But water spilled over the top of the *bulkheads* (walls), as it does over the top of ice-cube trays.

Twenty-five minutes after the *Titanic* struck the iceberg, Smith ordered officers to uncover the lifeboats

Women and children prepared to be loaded on the lifeboats. Many would never again see the husbands and fathers they left behind.

and begin loading passengers. Women and children were to go first. That was the rule of the time. The captain was sorry he had not held lifeboat drills.

Smith told officers in the radio room to call for help. They wired a ship called the *Californian*, about 10 miles (16 km) from the *Titanic*. But it did not answer. Its radio room was closed for the night. Another ship, the *Carpathia*, 58 miles (93 km) away, heard the call. The radio operator wired back, "Coming hard."

Water streamed into the lower part of the *Titanic*. Stewards told passengers to put on life jackets and come to the boat deck. First-class passengers grabbed their gold watches and diamond rings and other valuables. One man left thousands of dollars' worth of valuables and took four oranges.

Parents wrapped blankets around their children and carried them to the boat deck. People wore coats over pajamas. Some pulled on high-button shoes, and rushed off with them flapping open.

The crew took the covers off the lifeboats. Even if all sixteen wooden lifeboats and the four canvas ones were filled, a thousand people would be left behind.

The officers had trouble convincing people to get into the lifeboats. The *Titanic* was large and had bright lights. It seemed safe. The thought of dropping to the dark, icy ocean in a small open boat terrified many passengers.

The size of the *Titanic* made
it seem safer than the small
lifeboats. But it was the lifeboats that would stay afloat,
not the "unsinkable" *Titanic*.

The officers lowered lifeboats that were only half-full, because women and children stood back and refused to enter.

The wireless operators continued to call for help. First with the old *CQD*, then with the new *SOS* signal. Many ships answered, but none of them were close. The wireless operators hoped the *Carpathia* would come soon.

Captain Smith ordered rockets fired to let other ships know the *Titanic* was in danger. Men on the *Californian,* a few miles away, saw the rockets. But they did not radio the *Titanic* to see if they could help. When they told their captain about the rockets, he was not concerned.

Down in third class, water seeped into the cabins. Passengers tried to reach the boat decks above. During the first four days of the voyage, third-class passengers had not been allowed in the upper part of the ship. Now, many could not find the way there.

The *Titanic* listed more and more. The slanting position made it hard to launch the lifeboats. Now many passengers knew the *Titanic* was sinking.

Still, some women refused to go into the lifeboats. Mrs. Isador Strauss stayed to die with Mr. Strauss. Other women also chose to remain behind with their husbands.

As water climbed higher and higher, a few men

The tragedy of the *Titanic* was the big news of the day.

VOL. 35. NO. 5.   LAST EDITION   TUESDAY EVENING, APRIL 16, 1912.   FOURTEEN PAGES   PRICE ONE CENT

ONLY 868 ESCAPE

1,350 SOULS GO TO BOTTOM WITH HUGE LEVIATHAN TITANIC

Notables on Wreck

"Titanic," 1912

Date	Location	Fatalities	Remarks
4/15	North Atlantic	1,500	British liner *Titanic* hit an iceberg and sank. Hundreds of Americans perished. Worst Atlantic disaster.

The parishioners of Rosedale Methodist Church, in Winnipeg, Canada, were surprised. Their pastor of long standing, Reverend Charles Gordon, had been acting oddly all through the Sunday evening service. Now, instead of ending as usual, he wanted them to sing the hymn that went, 'Hear, Father, while we pray to Thee for those in peril on the

sea." Winnipeg, though surrounded by lakes, was not near the sea. Hudson Bay was more than 500 miles away, the Atlantic and Pacific much farther. What was the pastor thinking?

Even the pastor wasn't sure. He had taken a nap before services and had dreamed something very strange. All he remembered was the sound of rushing water, a sense of great excitement, and a tumult of voices—many voices—all requesting the hymn. Some urge made him ask the congregation to sing the hymn.

The night was April 14, 1912. More than 2,000 miles away on the Atlantic, a ship the size of a village, with a population to match, was indeed in peril on the sea. The Rosedale parishioners would always believe that despite the distance, the imperiled had sent them a message. They had answered it as best they could.

Apprentice John Gibson and Second Officer Herbert Stone of the freighter *Californian* had been standing on deck watching the huge ocean liner for over an hour. They'd spotted her at

Captain Edward J. Smith.

Titanic leaving Southampton waters for Cherbourg, first of two stops before crossing the Atlantic

tried to crowd into the lifeboats ahead of women and children. A man with a woman's shawl over his head slipped into a boat.

The bow of the *Titanic* dipped into the ocean, and the stern was lifted into the air. People climbed to the highest part and waited in terror. The band continued to play.

Finally the last lifeboat was launched. Fifteen hundred people were still on the *Titanic*.

The ship was almost standing on end. Furniture slid to the lower end and crashed. Some passengers and crew dived into the sea, hoping to be rescued.

At 2:17 A.M., the "unsinkable" *Titanic* began to slip into the ocean. People in lifeboats heard the screams of dying passengers. They watched the *Titanic* sink. Many saw their husbands or fathers drown.

Survivors waited in the icy darkness in the small boats. Finally, the *Carpathia* arrived. At 4:10 A.M., it picked up its first passenger from one of the lifeboats.

Men and women climbed a rope ladder to the *Carpathia*. Small children were put in sacks and baskets and pulled up by a rope. The *Carpathia* reached New York a few days later with 675 of the *Titanic's* passengers. Over 1,500 people had died in the Atlantic Ocean.

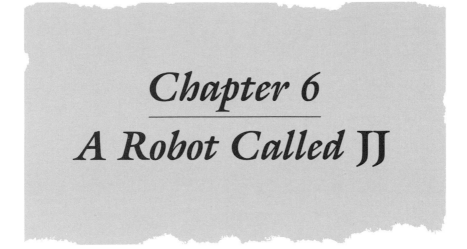

Chapter 6
A Robot Called JJ

Over the years, people have looked for the *Titanic*. In 1985, seventy-three years after it sank, American scientist Robert Ballard led a French-American search team. The team explored the area where the *Titanic's* lifeboats had been found in 1912.

In July of 1985, a French ship, carrying the French team and three Americans, searched with sonar. They saw no sign of the ship.

Then on August 25, an American ship hunted with video cameras. They loaded the cameras on a steel frame, which Ballard called *Argo,* and dropped them 2½ miles (4 km) below the surface of the water. *Argo* also carried sonar, still cameras, and other electronic equipment.

From their ship, Ballard and the other scientists

Finally, 2½ miles deep in the ocean, the *Titanic* was found.

from the Woods Hole Oceanographic Institution controlled the camera. They moved it back and forth over the ocean floor searching for the *Titanic*. Pictures taken underwater were flashed on a TV screen on their ship.

Members of the team of Americans and three French scientists took turns watching the screen. They saw hours and hours of mud. With only one week of the expedition left, they still had found no sign of the *Titanic*. After all his dreams of uncovering the *Titanic*, and all the expense, Ballard worried that they would not find the ship.

Then, about 1:00 A.M. on September 1, a picture of the *Titanic*'s boiler flashed on the TV screen. They had found it! The scientists shouted and laughed and slapped hands.

During the next few days, they took hundreds of pictures of the ship. They wanted as much information about the *Titanic* as possible. When they returned to Woods Hole, they planned an even more daring adventure for the following year.

In July 1986, Ballard's team returned to the spot where they had discovered the famous ship. They were going to travel to the bottom of the ocean to see the *Titanic* close up. Men would have to drop down nearly 2½ miles (4 km) into the ocean.

A different *submersible, Alvin,* would carry three men

and *JJ*, a swimming robot with a video camera as its eye. *JJ* was attached to *Alvin* by a line and was stored in a tiny garage on the submersible. The robot would go inside the *Titanic,* where it was too dangerous for human scientists to enter.

On July 13, 1986, Ballard and two other scientists squeezed inside *Alvin* and began dropping to the bottom of the ocean. Even before they finished the two-and-a-half hour ride to the ocean floor, they had problems. First, *Alvin*'s sonar, which guided them, quit working. They had to be led by sonar operating from the surface. Next, *Alvin*'s battery pack started leaking. They wouldn't be able to stay down long. Then the sonar guiding them from the surface went out. They had no way of knowing if they were close to the *Titanic.*

The men were ready to give up. But at the last minute the surface sonar began working again.

Now, the *Titanic* was only 50 yards (45.7 m) away. *Alvin* headed toward the ship. Suddenly Ballard saw black steel in front of him. It was the *Titanic*! The men looked at the ship briefly, then returned to the surface.

Two days later, *Alvin* landed on a deck of the famous ship. Martin Bowen guided the robot, *JJ,* inside the *Titanic* through the grand staircase. The men saw parts of the wonder ship. A chandelier still hung in the grand ballroom.

JJ explores the *Titanic* and goes where no
human has gone in more than seventy years.

The legacy of the *Titanic* even
inspired sideshows. Here's
an advertisement for the
Luna Park amusement park
at Coney Island, New York,
where the fateful accident
was reenacted for patrons.

Alvin's arm picks up a safe, which was probably emptied by the crew before the *Titanic* sank.

During the next week, Ballard and the others were constantly surprised. They found the ship's safe, and *Alvin* even picked it up with mechanical hands. They saw part of a doll that might have comforted a little girl, and china cups from which passengers might have been drinking tea when the ship struck the iceberg. They found pots and pans, and deck chairs. Boots stood upright in the bottom of the ocean.

These treasures from the past tell about life on the ship believed unsinkable—before it sank to the bottom of the ocean.

	Mary Rose	*Concepción*	*Titanic*
Year Sunk	1545	1641	1912
Type of ship	carrack warship	galleon	passenger liner
Where sunk	Solent, English Channel	Caribbean Sea	Atlantic Ocean
Near	Portsmouth, England	Dominican Republic	350 mi (563 km) SE of Newfoundland
How sunk	top-heavy, gunports open	caught on a reef	struck an iceberg
Lives lost	over 600	about 300	over 1,500
Discovered	1971*	1978*	1985
How deep	45 feet (13.7 m)	45 feet (13.7 m)	12,500 feet (3,800 m)
Raised?	yes (1982)	no	no
Search team director	Alexander McKee	Burt Webber	Robert Ballard

*Rediscovery

Glossary

Archaeologist—one who studies past peoples and cultures by studying objects they have left behind.

Astrolabe—an instrument used by pilots of seventeenth-century ships to calculate the position of the stars.

Bloodletting—allowing blood to run out of a sick person's veins.

Bridge—a platform above the main deck of a ship used by the commanding officer.

Bulkhead—a wall or partition which divides the ship into compartments.

Carrack—a large galleon.

CQD—a Morse code signal once used by ships in trouble at sea.

Crow's nest—a small lookout platform high on the mast or upright pole on a ship; can usually hold two people.

Deck—the floor of a ship; a platform going from one side of a ship to the other, or the space between two platforms.

English Channel—a part of the Atlantic Ocean that flows between England and France.

Gallant—brave, good, polite, and courageous.

Galleon—a large, high, three-masted sailing ship with three or four decks, used during the fifteenth, sixteenth, and seventeenth centuries.

Galley—a long, low, narrow fighting ship with sails and oars.

Gunport—an opening in a ship to allow a gun to be put through.

Knave—a mischievous or tricky person, scoundrel; sometimes a servant.

Listed—leaned to one side.

Magnetometer—an instrument used to locate metal underwater.

Piece of eight—an old Spanish coin made of silver.

Pike—a spear with a long wooden handle used in earlier times.

Reef—a narrow ridge of coral, rock, or sand near the surface of the water.

Scuba—from *S*elf-*C*ontained *U*nderwater *B*reathing *A*pparatus, and referring to an instrument which provides oxygen for underwater divers.

Sonar—from *SO*und *NA*vigation *R*anging, and meaning a system which finds underwater objects by reflecting sound waves off the objects.

SOS—a Morse code signal used by ships to call for help.

Submersible—a vessel which can operate underwater.

For Further Reading

Ballard, Robert. *Exploring the Titanic*. New York: Scholastic, 1988.

Brown, Walter and Norman D. Anderson. *Sea Disasters*. Reading, Mass.: Addison-Wesley, 1981.

Gibbons, Gail. *Sunken Treasure*. New York: Crowell, 1988.

Kraske, Robert. *The Twelve Million Dollar Note*. New York: Thomas Nelson, 1977.

Lampton, Christopher. *Undersea Archaeology*. New York: Franklin Watts, 1988.

Olesky, Walter. *Treasures of the Deep*. New York: Julian Messner, 1984.

Schwartz, Alvin. *Gold & Silver, Silver & Gold: Tales of Hidden Treasure*. New York: Farrar, Straus & Giroux, 1988.

Sloan, Frank. *Titanic*. New York: Franklin Watts, 1987.

Snow, Edward Rowe. *True Tales of Buried Treasure*. New York: Dodd Mead & Co., 1951.

Sobol, Donald. *True Sea Adventures*. New York: Thomas Nelson, 1975.

Sullivan, George. *Treasure Hunt: The Sixteen Year Hunt for the Lost Treasure Ship, Antocha*. New York: Holt, 1987.

Index

About the Author

Kathryn Long Humphrey grew up in Muscatine, Iowa, two blocks from the Mississippi River. The sights and sounds of barges and riverboats were an everyday part of her childhood. She studied at the University of Iowa, and wrote children's articles for the *Iowa Tests of Basic Skills* while earning her Ph.D.

Ms. Humphrey is the author of *Satchel Paige,* a National Council of Social Studies Notable book, and *Pompeii: Nightmare at Midday*. A school psychologist, Ms. Humphrey lives in Southern California with her husband, Dick, and two children, Richard and Jennifer.